First World War
and Army of Occupation
War Diary
France, Belgium and Germany

60 DIVISION
181 Infantry Brigade
Headquarters
5 October 1915 - 31 December 1915

WO95/3032/1

The Naval & Military Press Ltd
www.nmarchive.com
Published in association with The National Archives

Published by

The Naval & Military Press Ltd

Unit 10 Ridgewood Industrial Park,

Uckfield, East Sussex,

TN22 5QE England

Tel: +44 (0) 1825 749494

www.naval-military-press.com

www.nmarchive.com

This diary has been reprinted in facsimile from the original. Any imperfections are inevitably reproduced and the quality may fall short of modern type and cartographic standards.

© Crown Copyright
Images reproduced by permission of The National Archives, London, England, 2015.

Contents

Document type	Place/Title	Date From	Date To
Heading	WO95/3032/1		
Heading	60 Division HQ 181 Brigade Formerly 2/6 London Bde 1915 Oct 1915 Dec		
War Diary	Bps. Stortford	05/10/1915	05/10/1915
War Diary	Braintree	06/11/1915	05/12/1915
Heading	War Diary of 1st Infantry Brigade From 1st December 1915 To 31st December 1915 Volume I		
War Diary	Braintree	01/12/1915	31/12/1915
Heading	War Diary of 181st Infantry Brigade Machine Guns From 9th December 1915 To 31st December 1915 Vol 1		
War Diary	Braintree	09/12/1915	31/12/1915
Miscellaneous	181st Inf Brigade Machine Guns	18/12/1915	18/12/1915
Miscellaneous	General Idea	17/12/1915	17/12/1915
Miscellaneous	181st Inf Brigade Machine Gun Appendix 2	21/12/1915	21/12/1915
Miscellaneous	Tactical Scheme General Idea	20/12/1915	20/12/1915
Miscellaneous	Practise Mobilization Scheme Of 181st Inf Brigade Machine Guns	21/12/1915	21/12/1915
Miscellaneous	Brigade Major 181st Infantry Brigade	21/12/1915	21/12/1915
Miscellaneous	181st Inf Brigade Machine Guns Concentrate	21/12/1915	21/12/1915
Miscellaneous	181st Inf Brigade Machine Guns Orders For Concentration	21/12/1915	21/12/1915
Miscellaneous	Tactical Exercise 181st Infantry Brigade Machine Guns	30/12/1915	30/12/1915
Miscellaneous	Tactical Scheme	29/12/1915	29/12/1915
Miscellaneous	Brigade Tactical Scheme 181st Inf Brigade Machine Guns	31/12/1915	31/12/1915
Miscellaneous	Tactical Exercise 181st Infy Brigade	03/12/1915	03/12/1915
Miscellaneous	Appendix 1 General Idea		
Miscellaneous	181st Infantry Brigade Brigade Exercise December 2nd		
Miscellaneous	Test Mobilization Of 181st Infy Bde	22/12/1915	22/12/1915
Miscellaneous	181st Infantry Brigade	20/12/1915	20/12/1915
Miscellaneous	Appendix I		
Operation(al) Order(s)	181st Brigade Order No.2	21/12/1915	21/12/1915
Miscellaneous	Inspection of 181st Infantry Brigade by G.O.C 60th (London) Division	24/12/1915	24/12/1915
Miscellaneous	Officer Commanding 181st Infantry Brigade	20/12/1915	20/12/1915
Operation(al) Order(s)	181st Brigade Order No.1		
Miscellaneous	Programme For Inspection Of 181st Infantry Brigade	21/12/1915	21/12/1915
Miscellaneous	181st Brigade After Order	22/12/1915	22/12/1915
Miscellaneous	Programme For Inspection Of 181st Infantry Brigade	22/12/1915	22/12/1915
Miscellaneous	List Of Officers Who Will be Absent from Parade on 23rd December 1915	23/12/1915	23/12/1915
Miscellaneous	Officer Commanding	23/12/1915	23/12/1915
Miscellaneous	2/21st Battalion The London Regiment		
Miscellaneous	Tactical Exercise By 181st Infantry Brigade	31/12/1915	31/12/1915
Miscellaneous	General Idea		
Operation(al) Order(s)	181st Infantry Brigade Order No.1	29/12/1915	29/12/1915
Operation(al) Order(s)	181st Infantry Brigade Order No.2	30/12/1915	30/12/1915

WO 95/3032/1

60 DIVISION

HQ 181 BRIGADE
(FORMERLY 2/6 LONDON BDE)

1915 OCT — 1915 DEC

2904

Army Form C. 2118.

WAR DIARY
or
INTELLIGENCE SUMMARY.
(Erase heading not required.)

Instructions regarding War Diaries and Intelligence Summaries are contained in F. S. Regs., Part II. and the Staff Manual respectively. Title pages will be prepared in manuscript.

161 INF BDE

Place	Date	Hour	Summary of Events and Information	Remarks and references to Appendices
Bps. Stortford	5.10.15.		Reference Field Service Regulations, Part II, para. 140. 1. There is nothing to report. 2. The following points are noted. Remarks by Officers Commanding Units are attached in Appendices A. B. C & D. TRAINING. Progressing. The newly joined recruits are continuing to make progress. The number of untrained Officers is still a handicap to the Brigade. Efforts should be made to bring in trained and experienced senior Officers. Musketry is making headway although only in the preliminary stages as the practice Japanese ammunition has been withdrawn and there is no firing on the range. Facilities for training Machine Gunners has been augmented by the Divisional School being started, but the lack of guns with Units still militate against men being kept in training when once they have passed out of the School. The Brigade has been exercised in simple tactical schemes and on the 1st instant for the first time took part in a Divisional Concentration Scheme. DISCIPLINE. Good. ADMINISTRATION. 1. Medical Services. More Medical Officers are required to complete Brigade Establishment. 2. Veterinary Service. Good. 3. Supply Service. Good. 4. Transport Service. Improving. More wagons have been supplied during the month. There is still a lack of harness in some Units.	Appendices attached A. 2/21st Battalion London Regiment. B. 2/22nd Battalion London Regiment. C. 2/23rd Battalion London Regiment. ~~D. 2/24th Battalion London Regiment.~~

Army Form C. 2118.

(2)

WAR DIARY
or
INTELLIGENCE SUMMARY.

(Erase heading not required.)

Summary of Events and Information

5. Ordnance Service. Satisfactory.

6. Billeting and Hutting. The Brigade continues under canvas and the men seem comfortable and keep in good health. The water supply however is at times faulty. It would appear as if the supply pipe is too small for requirements.

7. Supply of Remounts. The Brigade is fully horsed.

8. Preparation of Units for Overseas. This is the ultimate object of the training. The number, however, of under aged recruits in the Brigade will have to be replaced and Units brought up to strength and trained before this Brigade could be sent on active service.

C. A. Noalli -
Colonel,
Commanding 181st Infantry Brigade.

Army Form C. 2118.

WAR DIARY
or
INTELLIGENCE SUMMARY.
(Erase heading not required.)

Instructions regarding War Diaries and Intelligence Summaries are contained in F.S. Regs., Part II. and the Staff Manual respectively. Title pages will be prepared in manuscript.

Place	Date	Hour	Summary of Events and Information	Remarks and references to Appendices
BRAINTREE	6.11.15.		Reference F.S.Regulations Part para. 140.	Appendices attached.
			1. There is nothing to report.	A. 2/21st Battalion London Regiment.
			2. The following points are noted. Remarks by O.C. Units are attached in Appendices A. B. C. & D.	B. 2/22nd Battalion London Regiment.
			TRAINING. Progressing.	C. 2/23rd Battalion London Regiment.
			The recruits continue to make good progress. The remark, last month, as to the number of untrained Officers being a handicap still applies. Musketry. Special attention has been paid in this branch, but without actual firing on the range, ammunition having been withdrawn. The Brigade has now 13 fully trained range finders against 5 last month. Machine Gunners. The Brigade has now 8 Officers and 75 O.Rs. fully trained as against 5 Officers and 39 O.Rs. last month. The Brigade has taken part in both the Divisional Manoeuvres and the Army Manoeuvres during the month, and the experience has been most valuable.	D. 2/24th Battalion London Regiment.
			DISCIPLINE. Good.	
			ADMINISTRATION.	
			1. Medical Services. More Medical Officers are urgently required to complete Brigade Establishment.	
			2. Veterinary Service. Good.	
			3. Supply Service. Good.	
			4. Transport Service. Improving. More drivers have been trained.	

1577 Wt.W10791/1773 500,000 1/15 D.D.&L. A.D.S.S./Forms/C. 2118.

Army Form C. 2118.

WAR DIARY
or
INTELLIGENCE SUMMARY.

(Erase heading not required.)

Place	Date	Hour	Summary of Events and Information	Remarks and references to Appendices
			5. Ordnance Service. Satisfactory.	
			6. Billeting & Hutting. The Brigade has been under canvas during the month and until the recent inclement weather the men have been comfortable and in good health. The Brigade is now in billets.	
			7. Supply of Remounts. The Brigade is practically fully horsed.	
			8. Preparation of Units for overseas. This is the ultimate object of the training.	
			C. N. Nowell, Colonel, Commanding 181st Infantry Brigade.	

Instructions regarding War Diaries and Intelligence Summaries are contained in F. S. Regs., Part II. and the Staff Manual respectively. Title pages will be prepared in manuscript.

Army Form C. 2118.

WAR DIARY
or
INTELLIGENCE SUMMARY.
(Erase heading not required.)

Instructions regarding War Diaries and Intelligence Summaries are contained in F. S. Regs., Part II. and the Staff Manual respectively. Title pages will be prepared in manuscript.

Place	Date	Hour	Summary of Events and Information	Remarks and references to Appendices
Braintree	5-12-15		Reference F.S.Regs.Part II.Para.140	A. 2/21st battalion London Regt.
			1. There is nothing to report.	B. 2/22nd battalion London Regt.
			2. The following points are noted.	C. 2/23rd battalion London Regt.
			Remarks by O.C.Units are attached in Appendices A.B.C.& D.	D. 2/24th battalion London Regt.
			TRAINING. Progressing.	
			The Recruits continue to make good progress. The remark last month, as to the number of untrained Officers being a handicap still applies.	
			Musketry. The Brigade has been issued with the .303 short Rifle and the Japanese Rifles withdrawn. Theoretical instruction in both Musketry and M.Gs. still makes satisfactory progress. Tactical Exercises have been much interfered with by the weather, nevertheless good progress has been made.	
			The Brigade establishment has been reduced to 25 officers and 500 rank and file. The transference of Supernumary Officers and men is in progress.	
			On 27.28.29.30-1-15 the Brigade was practiced in Extraining and Disentraining under Captain Saunders, 2/15th Bat.London Regt. It was satisfactorily carried out.	
			DISCIPLINE Good.	
			ADMINISTRATION	
			1. Medical Service. The villages of SIBYL HEDINGHAM and CASTLE HEDINGHAM placed out of bounds owing to Typhoid Fever.	
			2. Veterinary Service. Satisfactory.	
			3. Supply Service. Good.	
			4. Transport Service. Satisfactory. Unit's Limbered Wagons have been exchanged for the same number of G.S.wagons. A Motor Car has been placed at the Disposal of the Officer Commanding Brigade.	

Army Form C. 2118.

WAR DIARY
or
INTELLIGENCE SUMMARY.
(Erase heading not required.)

Instructions regarding War Diaries and Intelligence Summaries are contained in F. S. Regs., Part II. and the Staff Manual respectively. Title pages will be prepared in manuscript.

Place	Date	Hour	Summary of Events and Information	Remarks and references to Appendices
			5. <u>Ordnance Service</u>. There have been delays in execution of orders during the month.	
			6. <u>Billeting and Hutting</u>. The Brigade has been in good Billets during the whole month. The Billets of the Brigade were inspected on 21-11-15 and 22-11-15 by Colonel Davidson-Houston accompanied by the Sanitary Officer of the Central Force.	
			7. <u>Supply of Remounts</u>. Satisfactory.	
			8. <u>Preparation of Units for Overseas</u>. The employment of the Brigade in operations overseas is always kept in mind during all training.	
			C. L. Nicholl Colonel. Commanding 181st Infantry Brigade	

CONFIDENTIAL.

War Diary of
181st Infantry Brigade.
from 1st December, 1915 to 31st December 1915.
Volume I

Army Form C. 2118.

WAR DIARY
— OF —
INTELLIGENCE SUMMARY.
180st (Place heading not required.)
2/1st Infantry Brigade

Instructions regarding War Diaries and Intelligence Summaries are contained in F. S. Regs., Part II. and the Staff Manual respectively. Title pages will be prepared in manuscript.

Place	Date	Hour	Summary of Events and Information	Remarks and references to Appendices
BRAINTREE	1-12-15		Company and Platoon Drill under Company Commanders. Last hour Battalion drill.	fritz
"	2-12-15		Brigade Exercise. Route march taking tactical precautions to ABBOT'S HALL, each unit taking a different route. Brigade Drill carried out in the Park. Received:- 60:(Lon.) Div: C/132 forwarding VII Army letter 3A/C.R/240/A.Q re checking of secret documents.	Appendix "A" fritz fritz
"	3-12-15		Battalions take up an actual outpost line in country. Schemes arranged by O.C. Bn's HORLICK Captain J. H. Addokeam Guards takes over duties of Brigade Major vice Captain E. Marks 2/23rd London Regt who returns to his Bn=	fritz fritz
"	4-12-15		Units placed under C.O's for interior economy etc. Received:- 60th (Lon) Div: C/203/Q99 forwarding VII Army letter 3A/S.R/570/S.T re Motor Buses " " G.S/39(K) re Mobilization of Composite Brigade	fritz fritz
"	5-12-15	9 a.m	Church Parade	fritz

1577 Wt.W10791/1773 500,000 1/15 D.D.&L. A.D.S.S./Forms/C. 2118.

Army Form C. 2118.

WAR DIARY
INTELLIGENCE SUMMARY.
(Erase heading not required.)

Instructions regarding War Diaries and Intelligence Summaries are contained in F.S. Regs., Part II. and the Staff Manual respectively. Title pages will be prepared in manuscript.

Place	Date	Hour	Summary of Events and Information	Remarks and references to Appendices
BRAINTREE	6-12-15		2/23rd & 2/24th Bns furnish 200 men each under Capt ENGLISH 13 Bde Bombing Offr for digging Bde entrenching & bombing school. Company and Platoon Drill under Company Cdrs. Last hour Battalion Drill. Received:- 60th (Lon) Divn A/1517/16 re Officer establishment 2nd line Units. " " " C/132 re Secret Documents handed over on leaving Command III Army 115(B)	fultz
"	7-12-15		COLDICOTT Duties as for 6-12-15. Colonel H.S. Coldicott cdg 2/21st Bn London Regt to 3rd line Unit. Major B. FLETCHER takes Command.	fultz
"	8-12-15		Duties as for 6-12-15. Received from 60th (Lon) Divn C/71 re lights ahead of Official cars at night. A Party of 50 men working under the Bde Bombing Offr from 2/23rd Bn on entrenching a bombing school	fultz
"	9-12-15		Brigade Exercise cancelled owing to inclement weather. Units placed under Cdg Officers. Colonel C.N. WATTS cdg 181st Infy Bde on departure as President of a Court of Inquiry hands over Command to Colonel SIR THEODORE BRINCKMAN CB cdg 2/22nd Bn London Regt. 2/Lt C.C. ROSE 2/22nd Bn appointed ACTING BDE MACHINE GUN OFFICER. A Motor Car, driver and orderly Mr T. CUMMINGS arrived for Bde C O's use	fultz

1577 Wt.W10791/1773 500,000 1/15 D.D. & L.   A.D.S.S./Forms/C. 2118.

Army Form C. 2118.

WAR DIARY
INTELLIGENCE SUMMARY.
(Erase heading not required.)

Instructions regarding War Diaries and Intelligence Summaries are contained in F. S. Regs., Part II. and the Staff Manual respectively. Title pages will be prepared in manuscript.

Place	Date	Hour	Summary of Events and Information	Remarks and references to Appendices
BRAINTREE	10-12-15		Colonel C N WATTS on return resumed command of 181st Bde. Battalions take up Outpost Positions. Schemes arranged by O.C. Battalions. Received:- 60th (Lon.) Divn G/SQ0/A re discovery of illicit Signals, instructions on. " " " G/S 88/9 re Air Raids, instructions as to Kanomouv of intelligence. A M.G lecture to 6 Officers from each unit by Divisional Instructors at Bde. HQRS. BRAINTREE	
"	11-12-15		Units under Cdg Offrs for interior economy etc. Lt Col. H. NASH, The ROYAL SCOTS taken on strength of Bde.	
"	12-12-15		Church Parade.	
"	13-12-15		Company and Platoon Drill by Coy: Cdrs: last hour Battalion drill. Concentration Orders for COMPOSITE BRIGADE forwarded 60th (Lon) Divn with attached documents. The 4 M.G. Sections concentrates in BRAINTREE for training under Act: Bde M.G.O.	
"	14-12-15		Duties as for 13-12-15. STAFF-SGT ADAMS takes a class in physical training and bayonet fighting of Officers and NCOs of 2/23 & 2/24th Bns no 14th Dec -17th Dec.	
		8 PM	Telephone message received from Divn re expected ZEPPELIN raid.	

Army Form C. 2118.

WAR DIARY
INTELLIGENCE SUMMARY
(Erase heading not required.)

Place	Date	Hour	Summary of Events and Information	Remarks and references to Appendices
BRAINTREE	15-12-15		Units practiced under Battalion arrangements. Bde Cdr visits Bombing School at ONGAR.	initials
"	16-12-15		Route march under Battalion arrangements. Orders for Practice Mobilization Scheme issued to all units concerned. Brigade exercise cancelled owing to inclement weather.	initials
"	17-12-15		As for 15-12-15. Received:- 60th (Lon) Divn g/s 88/L a book of forms for reporting illicit signalling. 181st Bde: C97 forwarded Divn re shortage of men for training, returns of men unfit for foreign service	initials
"	18-12-15		Units under Offrs Commanding for Interior economy etc	initials
"	19-12-15		Church Parade	initials
"	20-12-15		As for 15-12-15. Lecture by Bde Cdr to officers on Order writing. Received:- 60th (Lon) Divn C/92a re 2/6th Lon: I.A. under Bde Cdr orders for mobilization & after. " " " G/357/1 re Position of Bde entrenching field, return of 6" map. IIId Army letter no 3A/364/6. etc Forwarded " " " 181st Bde S41 re lack of Communications connecting units of the Bde to Bde HdQrs. Course for Officers & NCOs at 2/21 St Bn COGGESHALL in Physical training & bayonet fighting. Commenced under Staff Sgt ADAMS 20th Dec - 23rd Dec	initials

Army Form C. 2118.

WAR DIARY
INTELLIGENCE SUMMARY.
(Erase heading not required.)

Instructions regarding War Diaries and Intelligence Summaries are contained in F. S. Regs., Part II and the Staff Manual respectively. Title pages will be prepared in manuscript.

Place	Date	Hour	Summary of Events and Information	Remarks and references to Appendices
BRAINTREE	21-12-15		Brigade Practice Mobilization Scheme. The actual march to STISTED PARK did not take place owing to inclement weather. Telegram forwarded TERRIFOR. CENTRAFORCE. III ARMY. DIVN HQRS re number of men fit for service overseas. Received:- HQtrs O.C. DIV: Train. Orders for ASC re mobilization of Composite Brigade.	Appendix #2 /ply /ply
"	22-12-15		Training under Battalion arrangements.	/ply
"	23-12-15		Inspection of Bde by G.O.C 60th (Lon) Divn. 3f a month sanctioned for expenditure on Bde Bombing School.	Appendix 3 /ply /ply
"	24-12-15		Units as per 22-12-15 Notices Received:- 60th (Lon) Divn G/S 39/P re orders to detachment of Cyclist Coy orders to accompany Composite Brigade	/ply
"	25-12-15		Christmas Day.	/ply
"	26-12-15		Church Parade	/ply

Army Form C. 2118.

WAR DIARY
INTELLIGENCE SUMMARY
(Erase heading not required.)

Instructions regarding War Diaries and Intelligence Summaries are contained in F.S. Regs., Part II. and the Staff Manual respectively. Title pages will be prepared in manuscript.

Place	Date	Hour	Summary of Events and Information	Remarks and references to Appendices
BRAINTREE	27.12.15		Holiday. Units trained under Battalion arrangements. Sniping in trench warfare.	July
"	28.12.15		Training under Battalion arrangements. Received:- 60th (Lon) Divn: G/593 re Cypher words. Telegram received from Divn: asking when drafts could be received. Lt Colonel PYLE Cdg 2/24th Bn & Major B. FLETCHER Cdg 2/21st Bn: leave for tour of inspection & instruction in FRANCE. Major HB DEWSBURY assumes command of 2/24th Bn: L.R. Major S. WRIGHT of 2/21st Bn: L.R.	July
"	29.12.15		O.o 26.12.15. M.g. lecture by Divn: School. Telegram from Divn: re telegram of 21st inst: as to in what particulars are officers not fully trained.	July
"	30.12.15		Brigade Tactical Exercise. The G.O.C. III Army & the G.O.C 60th (Lon) Divn: were both present. 2/Lt PHILLIPS 2/22nd Bn: appointed Bde Range Finding Instructor. Arrangements made for opening a Bde range finding school.	Appendix # 4 July

1577 Wt.W10791/1773 500,000 1/15 D.D.& L. A.D.S.S./Forms/C. 2118.

Army Form C. 2118.

WAR DIARY
~~INTELLIGENCE SUMMARY~~

(Erase heading not required.)

Instructions regarding War Diaries and Intelligence Summaries are contained in F. S. Regs., Part II. and the Staff Manual respectively. Title pages will be prepared in manuscript.

Place	Date	Hour	Summary of Events and Information	Remarks and references to Appendices
BRAINTREE	31.12.15		Battalions take up outpost positions. Schemes by O.C. Battalions. Lecture by Lt Colonel Lt. E.P. NASH on procedure in COURTS-MARTIAL.	July?
			Received :- 60th (Lon.) Divn. 3/C 59 report on Offrs & NCOs from entrenching fighting school KELVEDON.	
			" " G/5 39/Q re MGs & their ammunition for Composite Bde.	
			" " C/202/2/Q121 re issue of iron rations to Composite Bde. orders to 60th Divn. Train.	
			Forwarded " " 13De S/21/a/9. re irregularities of punishments in units.	
			The Col. Cdg. examined & passed Lt J.H. FIGG 2/24th Bn. in Coy. Drill for promotion.	

1577   Wt. W10791/1773   500,000   1/15   F. D. & L.   A.D.S.S./Forms/C. 2118.

CONFIDENTIAL

War Diary of

181st Infantry Brigade Machine Guns.

from 9th December 1915 to 31st December 1915

VOL 1.

Army Form C. 2118.

WAR DIARY
of
INTELLIGENCE SUMMARY.
(Erase heading not required.)

Instructions regarding War Diaries and Intelligence Summaries are contained in F. S. Regs., Part II. and the Staff Manual respectively. Title pages will be prepared in manuscript.

Place	Date	Hour	Summary of Events and Information	Remarks and references to Appendices
BRAINTREE	9.12.15		Training carried out in accordance with Battalion M. G. Section Programmes.	C.C.R.
"	10.12.15			C.C.R.
"	11.12.15		Church Parade	C.C.R.
"	12.12.15		2/21st & 2/22nd Sections arrived at BRAINTREE	C.C.R.
"	13.12.15		Consultation with Section Officers in regard to future training	C.C.R.
"	14.12.15		Training carried out in accordance with Battalion M.G. Section Programmes.	C.C.R.
"	15.12.15			
"	16.12.15		Inspection by Act. B.M.G.O. Brigade + Combined Drill; coming into action practised; Rearguard action in NOTLEY ROAD.	C.C.R.
"	17.12.15		Brigade Tactical Exercise "Attack"	Appendix 1. C.C.R.
"	18.12.15		Sections placed under Section Officers for interior economy etc.	C.C.R.
"	19.12.15		Church Parade.	C.C.R.
"	20.12.15		Brigade Tactical Exercise "Defence"; Observation Route March embodying concealment of guns	Appendix 2. C.C.R.
"	21.12.15		Practice Mobilization Scheme	Appendix 3. C.C.R.

Army Form C. 2118.

WAR DIARY
or
INTELLIGENCE SUMMARY.
(Erase heading not required.)

Instructions regarding War Diaries and Intelligence
Summaries are contained in F. S. Regs., Part II.
and the Staff Manual respectively. Title pages
will be prepared in manuscript.

Place	Date	Hour	Summary of Events and Information	Remarks and references to Appendices
BRAINTREE	22.12.15		Mechanism, Immediate Action, Preparation for Inspection	C.C.R.
"			Malthouse at WHEATSHEAF INN taken over as H.Q. of the B.M.G. for training in inclement weather & lecturing.	C.C.R.
"	23.12.15		Inspection of B.M.G. by G.O.C. 60th (LON) Div"	C.C.R.
"	24.12.15		Christmas Holiday with the exception of Interior Economy by Section Officers.	C.C.R.
"	25.12.15		Christmas Day	C.C.R.
"	26.12.15		Church Parade	C.C.R.
"	27.12.15		Christmas Holiday with the exception of Inspection of Arms by Section Officers	C.C.R.
"	28.12.15		Route March taking Tactical Precautions; a series of "Actions" being practised Section Drill, Semaphore; Mechanism	C.C.R.
"	29.12.15		Brigaded Tactical Exercise "Rearguard Action"	Appendix 4 C.C.R.
"			7 Riflemen returned to Battalion 2/21st Lon Regt. by order of the Brigade Commander for absence without leave.	
"	30.12.15		Brigade Tactical Exercise	C.C.R.
"			Letter received from Brigade Office Ref 5/20/6/12 from 60th(Lon)Div" G/539/9, 5/20/8/12 "Mortalysite"	Appendix 5 C.C.R.
"	31.12.15		Brigaded & Combined Drill; Mechanism; Lecture at H.Q. on "Barr & Stroud Rangefinder"	C.C.R.

1577   Wt. W10791/1773 500,000 1/15 D. D. & L.   A.D.S.S./Forms/C. 2118.

APPENDIX I

Tactical Exercise   17.12.15
181st Inf. Brigade Machine Guns.

The attached scheme was carried out by the Sections of the B.M.G. with fair success, but the lack of co-operation was noticeable.

C. C. Rose
2nd C.
act. B.M.G.O.

BRAINTREE.
18.12.15.

S C H E M E   No.1.

GENERAL IDEA.

Ref: Ord: Survey 1" Sheet 98.

The enemy strength about a Brigade of Infantry and 2 Battalions Artillery are holding a line on high ground from B of BECKERS GREEN to footpath about 300 yards north of V in VILLIUMS.

The G.O.C. 60th Division moving on BRAINTREE from BISHOPS STORTFORD orders the 181st Brigade supported by the 2/7th Brigade R. F. A. to take the position.

SPECIAL IDEA.

The 2/21st Section will advance due East from GOLDINGHAM FARM.

The 2/22nd Section will be in reserve at BUCKWOOD FARM.

The 2/23rd Section will advance due east from BUCKWOOD FARM.

The 2/24th Section will execute a flanking movement via THE MILL on the road BRAINTREE STATION to CHAPEL HILL.

The Artillery preparation will cease at 10 a.m. when the advance will be made by the 181st Infantry Brigade with Machine Guns providing Overhead Covering Fire.

The Infantry will re-organize for the final assault at 11 a.m. when the Artillery will resume to cover the advance of the Machine Guns in order that they can take up their positions for covering the final assault.

At 11.45 a.m. the final assault will be launched.

The assault being successful at 12 midday the 2/22nd and 2/23rd Sections will be rushed up to consolidate the position and the 2/21st and 2/24th will take up enfilading positions as a precaution in case the position is retaken by a counter-attack and the Brigade forced to retire.

                                            C.C.Rose 2/Lt.
                                            Act.B.M.G.O.

Braintree
17.12.15.

APPENDIX 2.

Tactical Exercise   20.12.15
181st Inf Brigade Machine Guns.

The attached scheme was carried out by the Sections of the B.M.G. with better result. The Co-operation & Inter-communication showed considerable signs of improvement.

C. C. Rose
2nd Lt,
Act. B.M.G.O.

BRAINTREE
21.12.15.

No. 2

TACTICAL SCHEME

GENERAL IDEA

Reference O.S. ½" Sheet 30

An enemy force composed of infantry, cavalry, and artillery, but strength unknown is advancing due East, from BISHOPS STORTFORD.

The G.O.C. 60 Division, moving West from COGGESHALL, orders, the 181st Infantry Brigade supported by the 2/7th Brigade R.F.A. to hold the BRAINTREE - WITHAM railway line, from the G of TYE GREEN to CRESSING Station, the flanks are protected.

SPECIAL IDEA

The 2/21st and 2/23rd Sections will take up positions on the high ground West of the BLACK NOTLEY - WHITE NOTLEY road.

The 2/22nd and 2/24th sections will be in reserve, but will take up positions on or near the railway line as a second line of defence.

The 2/21st and 2/22nd Sections have been allotted the right sector and the 2/23rd and 2/24th Sections the left.

BRAINTREE
20.12.15.

C. C. Rose
Lieutenant
A/Bde. Machine Gun Officer

APPENDIX 3.

Practise Mobilization Scheme
of 181st Inf. Brigaded Machine Guns   21.12.15.

The attached practise mobilization Scheme was satisfactorily carried out. Sections completed their mobilization well up to time. Sections mobilized on receipt of the order "Concentrate" issued at 6.30 A.M. The Brigade Office was informed that the B.M.G. had completed mobilization at 9.20 A.M.

Field Dressings & Iron Rations were not issued.

Inclement weather prevented the concentration at STISTED PARK. The B.M.G. marched to the "STARTING POINT" & returned to billets via CRESSING ROAD & CHAPEL HILL

C. C. Rose.
2nd Lt,
Act. B.M.G.O

BRAINTREE.
21.12.15.

To
    Brigade Major
      161st Infantry Brigade

Sir,
    I have the honour to report that the Brigade Machine Guns are ready to move off from their Alarm Post.
    I have the honour to be, Sir,
      yr obedient servant.
        C. C. Rose
          2nd Lt
        Act B.M.G.O.

BRAINTREE
21.12.15.
Time 9.20 A.M.

181st Inf. Brigade Machine Guns.

URGENT.

CONCENTRATE.

                                    C. C. Rose
                                    2nd Lt.

BRAINTREE.
21.12.15.   act. B.M.G.O
Time 6.30 p.m.
Sent to O.C. 2/21st Sect by orderly
  " " " 2/22nd "
  " " " 2/23rd "
  " " " 2/24th "

181st Inf. Brigade Machine Guns.
Orders for Concentration 21.12.15

Position of assembly STISTED PARK.
Sections will commence mobilizing immediately on receipt of order "CONCENTRATE"

Sections will be ready to move from the Alarm Post outside THE ROSE & CROWN at 9.30 A.M.

6.30 – 7.30 A.M.
   Pack kit-bags.
   Pack spare suits & caps separately.
   Roll, rope & label second blankets in tens.
   All the above to be taken to Co Stores.
   Officers kits to be taken by servants to Q.M. Stores.
   All water-bottles to be filled.

7.30 – 8 A.M.
   Breakfast.

(continued) 2.

9 - 9 A.M.
Packs to be packed, one blanket inside - Waterproof Sheet outside.
Iron Ration to be drawn
Field Dressing to be drawn.

9 - 9.30 A.M.
Fall In.
Distribute Ammunition 120 rds per man
Draw Haversack Ration.
March to Alarm Post.

One orderly per Section to report to B.M.G.O. at his billet at 6.A.M Address 86 HIGH STREET.

BRAINTREE 20.12.15.
Time 9.30 P.M.
Sent to O.C 2/21st Sect
  " " " " 2/22nd "
  " " " " 2/23rd "
  " " " " 2/24th "

C.C. Rose
2nd Lt
act B.M.G.O.

APPENDIX 4

Tactical Exercise   29.12.15.

181st Infantry Brigade Machine Guns.

The attached scheme was carried out by the Sections of the B.M.G in a satisfactory manner.

C. C. Rose
2nd Lt,
Act. B.M.G.O.

BRAINTREE.
30.12.15.

No.3

TACTICAL SCHEME

GENERAL IDEA

Reference O.S. ½" Sheet 30

Continuation of Tactical Scheme No.2

The enemy force being far superior as regards strength, the 181st Infantry Brigade Commander orders ~~the~~ retirement at 10.30 a.m. to the second line of defence on the Railway.

SPECIAL IDEA

At 10.30 a.m. the 2/21st and 2/23rd Sections will retire, gun by gun to the railway line where fresh positions will be taken up, during the retirement positions to cover the retreat must be taken up on the BLACK NOTLEY - WHITE NOTLEY road.

The 2/22nd and 2/24th sections will supply overhead covering fire during the retirement, the whole Brigade guns must be in position defending the Railway line by 12 o'clock mid-day.

BRAINTREE
29-12-15

E C Rose
Lieutenant
A/Brigade Machine Gun Officer

APPENDIX 5.

Brigade Tactical Scheme   30.12.15.
181st Inf. Brigade Machine Guns.

The attached scheme was carried out by the B.M.G. on arrival at GOSFIELD PARK. The Sections were bivouaced; horses outspanned, latrines dug; bounds given. The Sections were exercised in taking cover from aeroplanes & reassembling.
Dinners were then served, after which a Brigade movement was performed. The B.M.G. then bivouaced for 1 hour & then returned to BRAINTREE.

BRAINTREE
31.12.15

C. C. Rose.
2nd Lt.
Act. B.M.G.O.

APPENDIX I

Tactical Exercise 2-12-15
181st Infy Brigade

The attached scheme was carried out by the units of the Brigade with a fair amount of success. Brigade Drill was carried out in the Park, on arrival.

BRAINTREE
3-12-15

C. N. Watts. Colonel cdg
181st Infy Bde

Appendix 1.

GENERAL IDEA

1. A small raiding force (BLUE) has landed on the Coast between HARWICH and WALTON on the NAZE, and occupied COLCHESTER. Three Brigades of the Brown Force have been pushed forward to protect the Junction of Railways at MARKS TEY.

SPECIAL IDEA (BROWN)

1. On the evening of the 2nd December 1915, the O.C.BROWN Force receives orders that as another raiding party had landed the previous day at CLACTON, a halt of one day should be made to await arrival of further reinforcements.

xxxxxxxxx

181st Infantry Brigade

-----oOo-----

BRIGADE EXERCISE DECEMBER 2nd
---------oOo---------------oOo------

1. The Brigade will concentrate for drill on Thursday, 2nd December at ABBOTS HALL (1 mile South of SHALFORD) at 12.15 p.m.

2. POSITION OF ASSEMBLY - immediately South of the second gate of the North entrance to the Park; Adjutants and Brigade markers to report at that spot at 12 noon.

3. FORMATION - line of Battalions in Mass facing South in the order from right to left :-
    2/22nd   2/24th   2/23rd   2/21st
    The 2/6th Field Ambulance R.A.M.C. and No.4 Company A.S.C. will be on the left of the Brigade in the order named.

4. Battalions, the 2/6th Field Ambulance R.A.M.C., and No.4 Company A.S.C. will march by the following routes :-

2/21st Bn. London Regt	COGGESHALL - TUMBLER'S GREEN - BOCKING CHURCH STREET - GREAT CODHAM HALL - East Gate ABBOTS HALL.
2/22nd Bn. London Regt	DUNMOW - BLAKE END - GREAT SALING - SHALFORD GREEN - CHURCH END - North Gate ABBOTS HALL.
2/23rd Bn. London Regt	BRAINTREE - East Gate ABBOTS HALL (returning via SHALFORD GREEN and RAYNE)
2/24th Bn. London Regt	BRAINTREE - RAYNE - SHALFORD GREEN - CHURCH END - North Gate ABBOTS HALL (returning direct to BRAINTREE).
No.6 Field Amb. R.A.M.C.	BRAINTREE - East Gate ABBOTS HALL and return.
No.4 Company A.S.C.	Will follow the route taken by the 2/24th Battalion both on the out and return journeys.

5. Transport to be fully loaded each wagon etc. to have a card affixed shewing contents.

(sgd) E. SEABORN MARKS
Captain
Brigade Major
181st Infantry Brigade

BRAINTREE
29-11-15

APPENDIX 2

Test Mobilization of 181st Infy Bde 21-12-15

The attached Test Mobilization Scheme was quite satisfactorily carried out. All units completed their mobilization well up to time. Iron rations and field dressings were neither drawn nor issued.

The A.S.C owing to the large number of wagons employed on other necessary work did not parade.

Units mobilized on receipt, at 6.30 a.m, of the order "CONCENTRATE". The Bde office was informed by all units by 9.30 AM that all had been completed.

Owing to the inclement weather, the actual concentration at STISTED PARK did not take place. The Column marching as far as the STARTING POINT and returning to their billets. The 2/21st Bn received orders by cyclist to return to billets.

BRAINTREE.
22-12-15

C. N. Wells. Colonel
Cdg
181st Infantry Bde

Copy No.1.

181st INFANTRY BRIGADE

Order No.1.

SECRET.

CLOCK TOWER
BRAINTREE
20-12-15

PART I.

1. A Concentration of the 181st Brigade (less 2/22nd Battalion London Regiment) will take place on Tuesday 21. 12. 15.

2. Composition of Brigade:-

   Commanding   Colonel C. N. Watts

   Staff Officers   Brigade Staff

   Troops   Sect: 60th Div:Sig:Co:R.E.
                                  181st Infantry Brigade
                                    (less 2/22nd Bn.Lon.Regt
                                  181st Coy: A.S.C.
                                  2/6th London Field Ambce.

3. The Position of Assembly will be STISTED PARK.

4. Units will commence mobilizing immediately on receipt of order "Concentrate".

5. Alarm Orders will be acted on so far as they are not modified by Appendix I.

APPENDIX I.

Mobilization   5.30 - 7.30 a.m.

1st Hour.

Kits - Spare Clothing	1. Pack kit bags, convey same, spare kits (vide Operation Order No.8 Part II) and one blanket per man to Company Stores.
2nd Blankets.	2. Roll blankets in bundles (10) rope and label - fatigue parties.
Officers Kits.	3. Taken by Servants to Quartermaster's Stores.
Guard and Police.	4. Dismount Guard and Regimental Police.
Mobilization Boxes.	5. Pack Orderly Room Mobilization Boxes.
Rations.	6. Cooks prepare Haversack Rations.

7.30 - 8 a.m.

Breakfast.   Units will have breakfast.

8 a.m. - 9 a.m.

Transport Officer.
1. To send one wagon to Quartermaster's Stores to load Ammunition for distribution to Companies as per indents.
2. 2 Wagons (1 per 2 Companies) to load Blankets at Company Stores.
3. One Wagon to Quartermaster's Stores to load tools.
4. Two Wagons to Quartermaster's Stores to load Regimental Reserve Ammunition.
5. One Cart to load Officers Mess and Kits.
6. One Medical Cart to Battalion Headquarters for Stretchers, Medical Stores & Orderly Room Boxes.
7. Fill two Water Carts.

Fatigue Parties.   Fatigue parties as required to be detailed to load above blankets, ammunition, tools, Officers Mess and kits at Quartermaster's and Company Stores.

Dress.   Pack the Pack, one Blanket inside and Waterproof Sheet outside.

9 am - 9.30 am

Last ½ hour.
1. Fall in, distribute ammunition, issue Haversack Ration, march to Battalion Alarm Posts in order of march.
2. Report when ready.

J W Stowlick Capt
Bde Major
181st Infy Bde

Issued at
By
Copy No.1 Filed.
Copy No.2 60th (London) Division. *By post*
Copy No.3 Sect: 60th Divl. Signal Coy.   Copy No.8 O.C. 2/23rd Bn. L.R.
Copy No.4 Brigade Machine Gun Officer.   Copy No.9 O.C. 2/24th Bn. L.R.
Copy No.5 Senior Transport Officer.   Copy No.10. O.C. 181st Bde Coy.
Copy No.6 O.C. 2/21st Batt. London Regt. *By cyclist*   A.S.C.
Copy No.7 O.C. 2/22nd Batt. London Regt.   Copy No.11 O.C. 2/6th Field
By Post

All others by orderly

PART II.

Mobilization. 1. (a) All Units will be ready to move from their Unit Alarm Posts at 9.30 a.m.

    (b) Officers Commanding will report when they are so ready.

By Telephone or Telegraph in the case of the 2/21st Battalion London Regiment.

All others in writing.

Ammunition. 2. 120 on the Soldier   ) Calculated on present
100 in Regimental Reserve) state.

Tools. 3. As per Table II page 8 War Establishments T.F. 1915.

Blankets. 4. See Appendix I.

Rations. 5. Units will carry a Haversack Ration.

Transport 6. All available. Cookers will not be taken.

Rear parties 7. No rear parties are to be left with the exception of:-
    1 Quartermaster   )
    1 Orderly Room Clerk   )
    1 Junior Clerk   ) Per Battalion.
    1 Coy Q.M.Sgt. per Coy.   )
    1 Coy Storeman per Company)
    2 Cooks per Company   )
Other Units in proportion.
Will remain at Unit Headquarters.

Kit bags. 8. All kit bags will be packed and taken to Company Store Rooms where Orders will be issued regimentally as to their disposal. Second suits of uniform and spare caps, if any, will not be placed in the kit bags but will be stored separately in charge of the Company Quartermaster Sergeants.

Reports. Reports to Headquarters, 181st Brigade, BRAINTREE till 9.30 a.m., after that to the Head of the Main Body.

N O T E S.

2 Markers per Unit.   1. Adjutants and Markers of all Units (except
                                     Brigade Train) will meet the Brigade Major
Sect: 60th Divl.   at the WEST LODGE, STISTED PARK,
Sig: Co: R.E.   at 11 a.m. Markers as per margin.
1 N.C.O. only.

                            2. Adjutants will meet their Units at the
                               WEST LODGE, STISTED PARK (The Adjutant,
                               2/21st Battalion London Regiment will meet
                               his Battalion at The EASTERN LODGE, STISTED
                               PARK) and conduct them to their respective
                               positions.

                            3. Units after taking up position will
                               Bivouac. Pack animals will be unsaddled.
                               Teams outspanned. Latrines to be dug.

CRDER.

181st Brigade Order No. 2.

Ref. ½" Map   CLOCK TOWER
Sheet 30.   BRAINTREE
                                               21. 12. 15.

1. The Brigade (less 2/23nd Battalion London Regiment) will concentrate at STISTED PARK at 11.30 a.m.

2. The Starting Point will be Road Junction immediately WEST of the "B" in BRAINTREE.

Advanced Guard
Commander:
Major H.Dewsbury
Troops
2 Companies
2/24th Bn.L.R.

3. The Advanced Guard (Troops as per margin) will be clear of the Starting Point by 9.50 a.m.

Main Body.
Brigade Hdqrs.
Sect:60th Divl.
Sig:Co:R.E.
2/24th Bn.L.R.
(less 2 Coys)
Brigade Machine Guns
2/23rd Bn. L.R.
(less 1 Platoon)
2/6th Lon: Field Amb.
Brigade Train
181st Coy.A.S.C.

4. The Head of the Main Body (Order of March as per margin) will pass the Starting Point at 10 a.m.

5. Route BRAINTREE - JENKINS FARM - MILL - WESTLODGE, STISTED PARK.

Rear Guard.
Commander detailed
by O.C. 2/23rd
Bn.Lon.Regt.
1 Platoon 2/23rd
Bn.Lon.Regt.

6. The 2/21st Battalion London Regiment will concentrate independently.

7. Units Trains (less 2/21st Battalion London Regiment in order of March of Units will be brigaded under the command of Lieut. Dunn, 2/24th Battalion London Regiment.

8. Reports to Head of Main Body -

   After arrival at Position of Assembly to Brigade Headquarters, STISTED PARK.

                                               Captain,
                                               Brigade Major,
                                               181st Infantry Brigade.

Issued at
By
       Copy No.1. Filed.   Cyclist
8 pm   Copy No.2 to 60th Divn. by post 20.12.15.
  "   Copy No.3 to O.C. Sect: 60th Divl Sig:Co: R.E. by Orderly. 20-12-15
  "   Copy No.4 to O.C. Brigade Machine Gun, by Orderly.   "
9.30pm Copy No.5 to O.C. Brigade Train, by Orderly.   "
  "   Copy No.6 to O.C. 2/21st Bn.Lon.Regt.   )
8 pm   Copy No.7 to O.C. 2/23rd Bn.Lon.Regt.   )
  "   Copy No.8 to O.C. 2/24th Bn.Lon.Regt.   ) By Orderly.
  "   Copy No.9 to O.C. 181st Coy A.S.C.   )   "
  "   Copy No.10 to O.C. 2/6th Lon. Field Amb;   )   "

Appendix 3.

Inspection of 181st Infantry Brigade
by
G.O.C 60th (London) Division
23 - 12 - 15.

Owing to the state of the inspection & parade grounds, it was decided to parade the BRAINTREE and COGGESHALL units in the streets.

The G.O.C. 60th (Lon) Division inspected the units as per attached programme. whilst at BRAINTREE he interviewed Lt Colonel H. STREATFIELD and CAPT: E. MARKS of the 2/23rd Bn. LONDON REGT.

At COGGESHALL, he interviewed MAJOR B. FLETCHER, Cdg 2/21st Bn. LONDON REGT and also interviewed 2/Lt A. TEAROE of the same REGT.

The G.O.C 60th (Lon) Divn returned to BISHOPS STORTFORD at 4 PM

BRAINTREE
24 -12 -15

C. R. Watts. Colonel cdg
181st Infy Bde

COPY

2033

Officer Commanding,
181st Infantry Brigade.

The General Officer Commanding will inspect your Brigade on Thursday next the 23rd inst.

(1) Christmas leave for the 10% will not be stopped, but with that exception the Brigade will parade, as strong as possible, in marching order, with the Sginal Section, Field Ambulance, 1st Line Transport, and as many of the A.S.Corps Company as can be spared from their ordinary duties.

(2) Each unit will be inspected separately.

(3) Will you please submit a programme of time and place by 9 a.m. on Wednesday the 22nd inst, allowing half an hour for the inspection of each Battalion.

(4) If you wish him to take the Battalion at Dunmow en route, he would visit it at 10.30 a.m., and he could go on to Coggeshall at the conclusion of the inspection of the troops at Braintree.

(5) Please send with the programme, a list of all Officers who will be absent, shewing why absent and where.

(6) Parade states will be handed to him on the ground together with the following :-

    1 Name of Brigade Commander and Staff

    2 Names of Battalion Commanders, Adjutant and Transport Officer.

(sgd) C.S.Napier
Captain
General Staff
60th (London) Division

BPS STORTFORD
20-12-15

Copy No. 13

181st BRIGADE ORDER NO. I.

1. <u>The Brigade</u> (as per attached Programme) will be <u>inspected by the G.O.C.</u> 60th (London) Division on Thursday 23-12-15.

2. <u>Units with their 1st.Line Transport will be inspected</u> separately.

3. <u>The 2/21st Battalion and the 2/22nd Battalion London Regiment</u> will parade each on their <u>Unit Alarm Posts</u> for Inspection.
The <u>BRAINTREE</u> Units will parade on <u>the Brigade Bombing Ground, COGGESHALL ROAD</u>.

4. <u>Each Unit</u> on the conclusion of its inspection will march back to its Alarm Post and there dismiss.

5. <u>Officers Commanding Units at Braintree</u> will arrange that their respective Units are formed up in the COGGESHALL ROAD ready to take up position on the Parade Ground <u>without delay</u> on the departure of the Preceding Unit.

                                        Captain.
                                  Brigade Major.
                      181st Infantry Brigade.

Issued at

Copy No.1....... Filed.
"   " 2....... 60th(London)Division   by post 21.12.15.
"   " 3....... Sec.60th.Div.Sig.Co.R.E.   by orderly.
"   " 4....... 2/21st Battalion.L.R.   by post 21.12.15.
"   " 5....... 2/22nd   "   "   "   " 21.12.15.
"   " 6....... 2/23rd   "   "   "   " orderly
"   " 7....... 2/24th   "   "   "   "   "
"   " 8....... 2/6th.Lon.F.A.,R.A.M.C.   "   "
"   " 9....... 181st.Bde. Coy.A.S.C.   "   "

PROGRAMME

FOR INSPECTION OF 181st INFANTRY BRIGADE

on 23.12.15.

2/22nd Battalion London Regiment,   DUNMOW,   10.30 a.m.

Section 60th.(Lon.) Divnl.Sig.Co.R.E. BRAINTREE   11.45 a.m.

2/23rd Battalion London Regiment.   BRAINTREE   12. 0 noon

2/24th   "   "   "   BRAINTREE   12.30 p.m.

2/6th.London Field Ambulance   BRAINTREE   1. 0 p.m.

181st. Company A.S.C.   BRAINTREE   1.15 p.m.

LUNCH AT WHITE HART HOTEL, BRAINTREE.

2/21st Battalion London Regiment.   COGGESHALL   2.45 p.m.

For place of Inspection see attached orders.

                                        (sgd) C.N.WATTS
                                                      Colonel.
                                     Commanding 181st Infantry Brigade.
BRAINTREE
21.12.15.

Copy No. 11

181st BRIGADE AFTER ORDER.
----

1. This Order cancels 181st Brigade Order No.1, paras 3 (with regard to BRAINTREE Units) and 5, also programme as regards BRAINTREE Units.

2. Braintree Units will be drawn up for inspection in line as per programme attached. Transport in Column of Route.

                         [signature]
                         Captain,
Braintree.   Brigade Major,
22. 12. 15.   181st Infantry Brigade.

Issued at

Copy No. 1 ..... Filed.
"   " 2 ..... 60th (London) Division by post 22.12.15.
"   " 3 ..... Sec.60th.Div.Sig.Co.R.E. by orderly.
"   " 4 ..... 2/21st Battalion L.R. by post 22.12.15.
"   " 5 ..... 2/22nd   "   "   "   "   22.12.15.
"   " 6 ..... 2/23rd   "   "   "   " orderly.
"   " 7 ..... 2/24th   "   "   "   "   "
"   " 8 ..... 2/6th Lon.F.A.,R.A.M.C.   "   "
"   " 9 ..... 181st Bde.Coy.A.S.C.   "   "

PROGRAMME

For inspection of 181st Infantry Brigade.

on 23. 12. 15.

2/22nd Battalion London Regiment DUNMOW	10.30 a.m.
2/6th London Field Ambulance on The RAYNE ROAD BRAINTREE, facing WEST	11.45 a.m.
Brigade Machine Guns, MARKET SQUARE, BRAINTREE 2/23rd Battalion London Regiment, FAIRFIELD ROAD, BRAINTREE 2/23rd Bn. 1st Line Transport SOUTH STREET, BRAINTREE facing EAST	12.15 p.m.
181st Brigade Coy. A.S.C. SOUTH STREET, BRAINTREE, facing WEST	12.45 p.m.
2/24th Battalion London Regiment, COGGESHALL ROAD, BRAINTREE	1. 0 p.m.
Section 60th Divl. Sig: Co: R.E. COGGESHALL ROAD, BRAINTREE	1.30 p.m.

LUNCH AT WHITE HART HOTEL, BRAINTREE.

2/21st Battalion London Regiment, COGGESHALL	2.45 p.m.

All other instructions have been issued verbally to Units.

[signature]

Captain,
Staff Officer,
181st Infantry Brigade.

BRAINTREE
22. 12. 15.

LIST OF OFFICERS WHO WILL BE ABSENT FROM
PARADE ON 23rd DECEMBER 1915
----------oOo---------

2/21st Battalion

Captain	English	Brigade Bombing School
2/Lieut	Teuten	On leave
"	Reynolds	Divl. Instr. Machine Gun School
"	Liddiatt	" " Bombing School
"	Ockenden	Machine Gun Section
"	Tearoe	Reason Confidential
"	Nelder	Brigade Bombing School
"	Exall	3rd Army Trench Fighting School
"	Southin	Course of Musketry Bisley.

2/22nd Battalion

Major	Thompson	On leave
Captain	Colmar	3rd Army Headquarters
Lieut.	Grant	3rd Army Guard
2/Lieut	Hayford	3rd Army Guard
"	Allen	Sick leave
"	Brassey	O.i/c Rear Party Bps. Stortford
"	Phillips	Course Divl. Range Finding
"	Cartwright	Sick leave
"	Gane	Course Machine Gun, Bisley
"	Rose	A/Brigade Machine Gun Officer.

2/23rd Battalion

Captain	Cheek	Sick leave
"	Owen	Sick leave
2/Lieut	Mackay)	
"	Hunt)	Course of Instruction, Hertford
"	Wills	Course of Instruction, Camberley

2/24th Battalion

Captain	Harrison	Course of Instruction, Camberley
Lieut	Rees	Course of Instruction, Godstone
"	Holman	Leave
"	Pigg	Leave
"	Saville	Leave
2/Lieut	Goodyear	Course of Instruction, Oxted
Captain	Moss	Divl. Remount Officer.
Lieut	Palmer	Range Repairing Witham

2/6th London Field Ambulance

Nil

181st Brigade Company A.S.C.

Captain	Whittington	Supply Duty
Lieut.	Redwood	On convoy

Officer Commanding,
    2/23rd Battn. London Regt.
    2/24th Battn. London Regt.
    2/6th Field Ambulance
    181st Brigade Coy A?S.C.

    Especial care must be taken by O.C. units to prevent the blocking of civilian and other traffic during the G.O.C. 60th (London) Division inspection.

                        (sgd) J.N.Horlick
                                   Captain

BRAINTREE   Brigade Major
23-12-15   181st Infantry Brigade

2/23rd and 2/24th Battns.

    Drummers (without drums) and buglers will parade with their companies.

2/21st Battalion, The London Regiment

BATTALION COMMANDER	Major B. Fletcher
ADJUTANT	Captain A.J.Walter
TRANSPORT OFFICER	2/Lieut F.D.Levy

2/22nd Battalion, London Regiment

BATTALION COMMANDER	Col.Sir T.F. Brinckman Bart.,C.B.
ADJUTANT	Captain A.Mayer
TRANSPORT OFFICER	Captain H.Kitley

2/23rd Battalion, London Regiment

BATTALION COMMANDER	Lt-Col.H.S.J.Streatfeild
ADJUTANT	Captain H.Bateman Fox
TRANSPORT OFFICER	2/Lieut G.H.Baker (acting)

2/24th Battalion, London Regiment

BATTALION COMMANDER	Lt-Col.G.Elliot Pyle
ADJUTANT	Lieut. E.M.Greeff (acting)
TRANSPORT OFFICER	Lieut. E.S.Dunn

2/6th London Field Ambulance

OFFICER COMMANDING	Major J.E.B.Wells
ADJUTANT	Captain E.P.Minett (acting)
TRANSPORT OFFICER	Lieut. L.Wexthered

No.4 Company A.S.C.

Captain C.C.Smallwood.

---oOo---

Appendix 4

Tactical Exercise
by
181st Infantry Brigade
30 - 12 - 15

The attached scheme was carried out by The Bde on the date stated. The G.O.C III Army and the G.O.C. 60th (London) Division were both present at GOSFIELD PARK during the morning. The G.O.C 60th (Lon) Divn. again during the afternoon. The Units on arrival bivouacked & outspanned. Latrines were dug and bounds given. During the morning the G.O.C. 60th (Lon) Divn. ordered the troops to be put through an exercise in taking cover from aeroplanes & reassembling. This was carried out with success. After dinners the Brigade was exercised in Brigade drill by the Bde Cdr. At 3 P.M. the Brigade left on its return journey. During which 5 men fell out from the 2/21st Bn London Regt on their way to COGGESHALL. 1 man only from the units returning to BRAINTREE

BRAINTREE
31-12-15

C. U. Watts. Colonel
cdg
181st Infy Bde.

GENERAL IDEA

Reference O.S. ½" No. 30, and any map of Eastern Counties.

    KHAKI Home Defence Troops are moving Northwards to the line CAMBRIDGE - IPSWICH to resist the advance on LONDON of a GREY invading force, which has landed on the NORFOLK COAST.

SPECIAL IDEA ----- KHAKI FORCE

    The 60th. (London) Division is ordered to concentrate at HAVERHILL on the COLCHESTER - CAMBRIDGE Branch Line of the G.E. Railway.

Copy No.

181ST. INFANTRY BRIGADE   Order No. 1.

BRAINTREE
29th. December 1915.

Reference O.S. ½" No. 30
& any map of Eastern
Counties.

1. (a) A Grey Invading Force which has landed on the
    NORFOLK COAST is moving on LONDON.
   (b) The 60th. (London) Division is ordered to
    concentrate at HAVERHILL as part of a
    movement of Home Defence Troops to resist
    the enemy's advance.
2. The 181st. Infantry Brigade (less the 2/22nd
   Battalion, London Regiment) will concentrate at GOSFIELD PARK to-morrow en route
   to HAVERHILL. Rendezvous Eastern Entrance
   of the Park.
3. The 2/22nd. Battalion, London Regiment will stand
   fast at DUNMOW with special orders (imaginary
4. The 2/21st. Battalion, London Regiment will march
   at 8-45 a.m. the 30th instant and follow the
   route COGGESHALL, HOVELS FARM, TUMBLERS GREEN
   STISTED RECTORY, BOULTWOODS FARM, ROMAN ROAD.
5. The Troops in BRAINTREE will march at 10 a.m., at
   which hour the head of the main body will pass
   the Starting Point.
6. Starting point The MILL in BOCKING.
7. Advanced Guard, composition as in margin.

Advanced Guard
Commander Major Dicks.
2/23rd. Lond. Regt.
Signal Section R.E.
One Company 2/23rd.
Lond. Regt.

Order of March
Brigade Machine Guns
2/23rd. Lond. Regt.
(less one Company)
2/24th. Lond. Regt.
Eschelon B. First Line
Transport under command
of Senior Transport
Officer.
No. 6 Field Ambulance
Battn. Trains in order
of march of Units.
181st. Brigade Coy. A.S.C.
The trains and the A.S.C.
under command of O.C.A.S.C.

8. Main body, order of march as in the margin.

9. Reports to head of main body.
10 Further orders will be issued at the rendezvous.

[signature]
Captain,
Brigade Major,
181st. Infantry Brigade.

Issued at   a.m.
Copy No. 1 Filed.
" No. 2 Divl. H.Q.
" No. 3 2/21st. Bn. Lond. Regt.
" No. 4 2/22nd. Bn. Lond. Regt.
" No. 5 2/23rd. Bn. Lond. Regt.
" No. 6 2/24th. Bn. Lond. Regt.
" No. 7 O.C. 2/6th. Field Ambulance.
   No. 8 181st. Coy. A.S.C.
   No. 9 O.C. Sig. Coy. R.E.

Copy No.

181ST. INFANTRY BRIGADE   ORDER NO. 2

Reference ½" Manoeuvre
Map Sheet 30.

Rendezvous
EAST GATE
GOSFIELD PARK

30-12-15.

1. The Brigade will halt for dinners till 2 p.m.

2. Battalions and attached Units will form in mass facing West S.W. of EAST GATE in following order from right to left:-

   Brigade Machine Guns.
   2/21st. Battalion
   2/23rd. Battalion
   2/24th. Battalion
   2/6th. London Field Ambulance.
   181st. Brigade Coy. A.S.C.
   2nd. Echelon 1st. Line Transport and Battalion Trains will join their Units and form up in rear of them.

3. Adjutants and Brigade Markers will report to Brigade Major at EAST GATE at 11-40 a.m.

JMNick
Captain,
Brigade Major,
181st. Infantry Brigade.

Issued at
Copies to

No. 1 Filed
2 Divl. H.Q.
3 2/21st. Bn. Lon. Regt.
4 2/22nd. Bn. Lon. Regt.
5 2/23rd. Bn. Lon. Regt.
6 2/24th. Bn. Lon. Regt.
7 O.C. 2/6th. Field Ambulance.
8 181st. Coy A.S.C.
9 O.C. Sig Coy R.E.

www.ingramcontent.com/pod-product-compliance
Lightning Source LLC
Chambersburg PA
CBHW081454160426
43193CB00013B/2477